Blue Lotus

*Poetry * Quotes* Poetic Prose*

- Blue Lotus -

Leanne Neill
LUST for WORDS

Blue Lotus

Copyright © 2018 Leanne Neill
All Rights Reserved
ISBN 978-1-925332-39-1

Cover designed by
L. Neill and M. Gregory

Cover Image:
© Trevoux/Dreamstime.com

Internal illustrations:
© Can Stock Photo Inc. / mystocks

This book may not be reproduced, transmitted, or stored in whole or in part by any means, including graphic, electronic, or mechanical without the express written consent of the author except in the case of brief quotations embodied in critical articles and reviews and non-commercial uses permitted by copyright law.

For permission requests, address the request to the author c/o Permissions,
jneill@bigpond.net.au

Printed in Australia

Publisher of record
Tried and Trusted Indie Publishing
www.tatindiepublishing.com

ACKNOWLEDGEMENTS

For Rachel:
rising from the ashes valiantly with her red hair,
to my blue lotus.
Always X

If I have ever
loved you,
please know,
I still do X

Leanne

CONTENTS

Sedation.............1

Aphrodisia......45

Euphoria..........81

- Blue Lotus -

PREFACE

Planning
to write
my
memoir
on
a postage stamp.

*She didn't say
an awful lot,
but a few
pretty words
went a long way…*

©Leanne Neill

SEDATION

Empath's Ode

I beg of you
not to give me
your pain.
I shall assume it
as my own
garment,
laden with your angst;
dragging coattails
behind,
removing any traces
of blood.

Compliance

Snug overcoat;
cohesive patches,
threadbare places.
Shoes once too tight,
distended,
loosely compliant.

Stripped of shame
by the comfort
of indignity,
you
triumphantly wore
my
resolve.

*It must be easy not to look within,
when you don't own your reflection.*

Daddy's Girl

When you
were born,
not one night
of reprieve.
Nurses
wheeled you back;
*she's all yours,
this one
can't be pacified.*

Thirteen years on,
still you can't
be tamed.
I cannot
appease you.
Fitting;
Daddy's girl.
He wanted you,
before me.

*Watching my essence dissolve,
as I give you life.*

Sundays

I never liked
Sundays.
The night
equaled
a melancholy
only met
by Monday,
when all
the monsters
I had imagined,
came to be.

She always felt sad;
sometimes she just pretended,
to make others happy.

Sedation

When Dove Cries

This house,
always so cold,
stark, white
in the latest
Home Beautiful
way.

The tin called it
Dove...

Fireplace hints
of warmth,
cosy nooks
suggest comfort,
framed faces
hang by jovial
smiles.

S t i l l
it echoes...

Lonely hearts
splinter,
piercing in regret,
blood lines
failing
their path
home.

Next time,
Olive...

Disillusion

Remember when
we believed?
God, ghosts,
Santa Claus,
the tooth fairy;
tales of cheesy
man-on-the-moon
made dreams.

Conspiracy
closes in,
disillusion stifles
with horrid
insistence.
All too distinct;
we're not
who we used to be.

Best Friend
(for Rachel)

Little girl;
red hair,
smattering of freckles.
Offering
your free spirit
to my complex olive skin,
as we moulded sandcastles
and plasticine.

Entwined
through life's absences;
miles between.
Losing boys,
family, babies,
husbands.
Sinking simultaneously,
it always seemed.

If I could take your pain
I would;
twists of fate
putting you in shoes
I should be wearing.
I feel it just the same.
I love you.

Vulnerable

There are things
that never change.
Insecurity bred
in childhood
reaches fruition
in adult time.
Absent *I love you's*
from those who rear,
ensure an early ticket
to incarcerated freedom
from the first to profess,
and a profound lifetime
of vulnerability,
ever after.

Familiar Festivity

Let us
skim
stagnant surfaces,
so as not
to draw blood.

One sitting
on the spectrum,
somewhere between
Narcissus
and Mr. Asperger,
entertaining herself
as usual.

Troublemaker
simmering
new plot twists,
as the rest
refuse to believe
there's no goodness
bubbling beneath.

Newly loved-up
opposite;
having again
forgotten,
monogamy
is a lie...

Progeny
skip
to the innocence
of a scary fat man's
promises;
his Missus helping,
as she should.

Nobility
at head of the table,
overseeing calamity
with the bias
only genetic wisdom
curtails.

Poet
swatting in the corner,
itching madly,
from the moment
she blew in.

Sedation

Black Sheep

I care less
if blood is thicker than water,
it coagulates and sticks
like shit to your shoe.
There's always one
whose DNA reeks of the postman,
I hope to God, it's mine.

*You'll never amount
to more than a big fat nothing;*
mud you threw to blacken
from your golden fleece.
I can't thank you enough,
I'm my own big sister now.
I've almost wiped my soul clean.

Perfection

I'm tired
of being
so articulate.

Noticing
the spots
on the rug
match the
border in
the artwork.

While he fails
to notice
I walk by unclothed,
I see
the turquoise in his tie,
exactly reflect his eyes.

How instead,
your complexion
complements
my exhausting
constitution,
perfectly.

Weary Stars

Even stars grow weary;
competing for stellar position,
to shine the brightest,
be identified by name.
Twinkling in rhyme,
falling upon your every wish.
There's only brief respite
behind clouds before the sun rises,
insistent on its near radiant
supremacy.

*She often tried obscurity;
it just didn't suit her.*

Rest in Truth

She was kind,
though tended
to bitch.
She didn't judge
unless
they didn't agree.
The perfect mother;
begrudging quietly
every small sacrifice.
Most thoughtful wife;
driving him underground,
first.

As I repose
in my velvet-lined
sanctum,
please don't canonise
me.
I'll be unconsciously aware;
you know damn well
I never miss a beat!
Tell it simply,
as it was.
Lay me deeply,
in my own honesty.

When All is Nothing

My only
respite
is in
closed eyes,
when
consciousness
meets oblivion.

I imagine
it as death;
before birth,
when all is nothing,
though exactly
as I exist,
with eyes open.

Just a dreamer in a broken sleep...

Dancing Ashes

You
died
that day,
after
promising
so long.

I
just wasn't
meant to be left
carrying
your ashes
dancing.

*How to stop this deluge of drowning,
this aching of alone,
this complete missing of you,
without me?*

Questioning the Dead

Carved earth,
fresh grooves;
perfect
rectangular
symmetry.
Six feet deep;
how can anyone
really be sure?
Just as I questioned
throwing that rose
upon you,
eyed that sardonic
bobcat machine
staring in wait,
and felt smugly
satisfied,
you weren't in there.

For every moment thinking I no longer miss you,
I spend a lifetime wondering why you left.

No Jacket Required

Many times
I've needed you;
unavailable,
inaccessible,
and so,
I've withdrawn,
don't dare ask
for any of your pieces.

Keeping all at bay,
running in my own circles
to keep warm.
You say I've become
incredibly resilient;
we both know
that's just a complimentary
synonym for *cold*.
As long as I'm out of your hair,
no jacket is required.

Almost funny...
The way I pretend
I don't need you,
the way you believe me.

Stitches in Time

Holding hands
along the foreshore,
undeterred by props
of a long time.

Silver threads
hemming them
firmly together,
against
changing tides.

I can't help but wonder
why we now
allow the waves,
to prematurely
unpick our stitches.

*Well-worn track,
threadbare in places.
Your apologies as fleeting,
as my heart is quick.*

Away

I felt
the tide
change.

Salt air
bruise
my lungs.

Long before
they
carried you.

*I miss you
in love
with me...*

Leaving

Drawing
the shutters
tight,
rapping
my knuckles
without
remorse.
Clicking
goodbyes
beneath
your tongue;
above
your breath.

I never
did know
when
to leave.

*You were not my life.
Only 1,263 days,
that no longer count.*

Blue Lotus

Mute

Sudden stillness,
where usually
a constant roar.
Nothing even whispers;
whimpers of transient words,
impossibly strung.

Perhaps
I've finally polished
all the pieces.
Only so many boulders
you can overturn,
before left naked;
buried beneath
an avalanche of vulnerability.

Pity the masochistic poet;
harmonising lines of pain relief
whilst constantly reliving them.

By Stealth

Sleep,
I avoid you,
in the quiet of darkness
by stealth.
Monsters under my bed,
teeth sharp and defined.
Even the certainty of daylight
allows no comfort,
in your shadowed bruising.

*Tried to cry, felt that familiar quake inside.
Skipped some meals, a night sleep;
seems, the pipes have all burst...*

Cocoon

Spinning
in my silk haven.
These walls know
my virtues,
forgive my sins,
judge me
not by my vices.
Cocooned in myself,
would you even care
to notice
if I didn't come out
today?

*I prefer anonymity in the real world;
everything else is just a farce...*

Sedation

Survival

Survival
kicks in.
Chest rises
in rhythm,
heart beats
on repeat;
involuntary
mechanism
of self-defence,
unperturbed
by any lack
of reason.

*I've learned
if I turn
myself
inside out,
I can
disappear.*

Rain

The rain
has been slight,
in defiance
of winter.
I can't help but wonder
if it's made you
sad.

Today
it concedes,
in spiraling sheets.
You love the rain.
I imagine you
cocooned safely in yours,
feeling better.

Converging perspective of melancholia.
Inextricable.
Raindrops on my window, teardrops in my eyes.

Unkept

I must forget,
but I don't
want to
and last night
you woke me,
short of my own
breath.

Your edges
had faded
but I recognized
you,
were no longer
my,
decision to keep.

Dawn arrives;
day conscious,
without you...

Secrets

To my grave
I will take us;
heart and mind,
ashes into dust.
Unless the wind blows
in an unknown direction,
no one
will ever guess,
I lived only for you.

Festering grief;
it's only my corpse
decomposing.

Disintegration
is a timely process;
soon enough,
we will both disappear.

Enlightening

Another year
passing,
without you.
I feel the next
milestone approaching,
before I'm ready.
Your old soul
never ages your face
in real time.
Will we ever catch up?
Not in this life...
I allow the weight
to stop bearing
on my chest;
such a sorrowful
lightening.

*It scares me,
I no longer miss you;
it was everything
we had left.*

It's Complicated

My eyes
have seen,
become narrow.
My skin worn,
too many summers.

Only natural
you should leave;
wide-eyed,
complexion
still so pale.

I envy all you lack.
No time to feel;
it's a busy life.
No shades between
black and white;
all is cut and dried.

Tripping

Tripping
over
the loss
of you.

Always
clumsy
as can be.

Stumbling
over things,
that aren't
even there.

She looks lovely, dressed in my goodbye...

Distance

This distance
lapses between us,
warping our touch,
fading our memory.

Bridging the gap
takes two hearts aligned.
We incline to fear,
both going under.

*Don't think for one moment
those sweet messages sent from afar,
compensate for your lack of wanted presence
in the here of now...*

Sedation

Again

Farewell
once again.
Sunlight insists
on penetration;
earth, rotation.
Mandatory
slow-motion;
unaware,
without you.

Can't you hear my heart squeak,
every time you leave?

Left of Me

All that time
teaching you
to believe
in yourself,
never realising
once I succeeded,
there would
be nothing left
for me.

*How shrewd you were;
convincing me
in life there is only pain,
then running away
with all my former optimism.*

Sedation

Surrender

She's pretty
in that effortless
kind of way;
no time wasted
cosmetically
enhancing.

Youth
on her side,
no need to meet me
in any corners,
fists flailing.

Hands up,
hands down,
she's going to win.
I've become
irrelevant.

Holding On

In one hand
she held her
bleeding heart,
in the other,
she held the
weeping world.
In between
the two,
she was barely
holding herself
together.

If I'm to die soon, take my heart.
Gift it only to an old person;
they'll know how it works.

Your Will
(for Dad)

You bestowed
secret codes
that made you sad,
made you mad,
drove you to placate
everything bad.

Intrinsically
encrypted,
I am
your daughter.

Defunct

I feel
my womb
shriveling,
weeping orifices
provide
no rehydration.

My
hips and thighs
thickening;
some kind of
unnecessary
rebellion.

As if
my head
is not
already heavy,
just holding
itself up.

Too Good at Goodbyes

Tears
dry
in haste,
barely
tumbling
to my
cheek.

Meandering
alternative
paths,
deviating
trails
of
goodbye.

*I've died for you so many times,
surely once more won't kill me?*

No Prisoners

Not sure which is greater?
The lump in my throat
I leap to swallow,
or the laden stone,
unskimmable,
weighting my chest.

They both
threaten to steal my breath,
take me under.
No prisoners,
equally insurmountable.

Again, I have spent today missing...

Still Blue

It's not
the same
here now.

Water
still blue
as the sky.

Tainted chill
that parts my tendrils -

in waves
of unruly
goodbye.

*A teen when I first contemplated my demise -
by my own hand,
through
unwanting eyes.*

Parasite

Under my skin;
infusing bloodstream,
pervading parasite.
Burrowing deeper,
imbedding,
morphing into one.
Unskimmable surface,
intrinsic essence,
integral lifeforce.
Whispering,
talking,
screaming.
I'll pass quietly;
nothing left
to say.

*Back to what I knew before you;
nothing looks the same.*

Sedation

The Sun Will Break

As the light descends,
I slip into a murky hiatus.
My old friend is knocking;
to answer, is to be at home.

My head barren,
devoid of thought.
My heart haemorrhaged;
feel your teeth sink, as it deflates.

My body splintered, particles and shards;
dust, no place to rest.
My bandage unraveled,
tourniquet come loose.

I catch a glimpse into the distance.
Just a twinkle, enough to sting my eyes.
Somehow, I recall,
the sun will always pierce the black.

APHRODISIA

Man of Colours

Abstract portrait,
splashes and swipes.
Stroking crimson flushes,
tending to moods
of blue and grey.
You bleed into one;
my fingers swirl through.
I can again see beneath;
my man of colours.

I won't keep digging to find you.
Buried treasure is cumbersome to exhume.
Too much mud now, beneath my fingernails.

Bound

Indiscernible
rings of growth;
no measure
by years
or weather.

You and I
infinitely bound,
before
the marking
of time.

*Our bodies
move
in perfect rhythm
to the sound
of our hearts,
beating
as one.*

Cover Me

Cover
my eyes,
spin
me around.
Align
yourself
with a million
others.

I know
the sound
of your
heart...

It took half to find you;
next half,
lost without.
Entirely,
the love of my life.

Compulsion

You stopped
to ask
if I was okay.
I smiled coyly;
so we continued
our rhythmic slide
into what
we both knew
would be the most
compelling
destruction.

*You were an impending fiasco,
impersonating a thrilling adventure.*

Flesh

You
crawled
into that
space
between
skin
and bone,
gnawing
the only
part of me
held
together.

*We were so effortless;
even those first few butterflies sat quietly
in reverence.*

Bargaining Power

Your loyal disciple,
hanging on every word;
you gift them
selectively,
as a wise man
grants falling stars.

I've always been one
to settle
for a bargain,
even if my heart is appeased
at the expense
of reason.

*I don't like getting wet.
For you, I'd cross oceans,
and make it my pleasure.*

Aphrodisia

Fickle

Arid, this cruel land.
Load breaking my back,
left ankle bone jutting
from flesh.
Fallen; one too many cracks.
This pain not distinguished
from another.
Slithering on my belly
towards your distance.
Lushness of palm trees,
liquid-lust oasis.
Fanned by large fronds,
faithful followers polish
your crown.

Its glint blinds clarity of vision,
though appeals to my fickleness.
I'm conscious of the mirage;
still, I die to meet you.
Arriving at your altar,
melting to replenish your insatiable
thirst.

You smile as you sip your Pina Colada,
spinning a paper parasol,
between your gold-capped teeth.

Do You Remember?

Remember
that morning,
before we said
goodbye,
not knowing
it was our last?
We swam
in each other's
eyes,
and when we said,
you're the love of my life,
we both believed it.

*I miss the way our bodies melded,
so that your heartbeat fit perfectly into my ear.*

She Wins Every Time

I loved to watch
you write...

Frantic spin
of razor sharp wheels;
veering,
ceasing
not even for sleep.

Possessed by rotation;
remoulding my eyes
dizzy green,
as she dominated
you
over
me.

Still,
we
became
immortalized;
blood lovers,
fingers smudged
together.

Only when
I
leapt from ink
in a rebellious
state of reality,
did
your
cogs stop turning.

It was then I knew,
I could never compete...

Clapped Out

How many
hearts
you quietly
entertained,
while mine
believed
it was the only
one
in the audience.

*Make no promises you can't keep.
I'd rather see you weak, than a liar.*

On Top

Preferable
wasn't it?

Salted caramel,
tip of your tongue,
me beneath,
catching drips.

You never did
like me on top.

*I swear after all this time,
I can still taste your poetry on my fucking lips...*

Reap

Don't try
to ride
on my coattails.

Sown
with my own
blood and sweat.

I've not yet
reaped
of my flesh.

*Her delicacy one could only dream
of entangling.*

Scars

I
marked
my skin
today,
in permanent
ink.

I
always
wanted you
to believe
I was cool.

I
wasn't quite
brave enough,
to use
a knife.

Manipulator of love;
I never could bend to fit
the distortion of your heart.

All of Me

Could
we just
pause that night,
when Earth
lost orbit?

I offered
all of me,
you took it,
at last.

Time though
never
stands still,
even when
most precise.

Hearts pill
with friction;
in turn,
everything
must change.

Shhhh...

Give me
that golden
silence
from your lips,
it's far
less abrasive
than your
sandpaper tongue.

*Your mouth professed a vow your hands
could never keep.*

Age-old Questions

How will I know
when I don't turn you on?

When my sensuality disfigures,
morphs in to that old lady
you despise.

When they're flitting around you,
shining their tight bodies,
loose minds.

When I'm forgetting who I am
and you're just learning
yourself.

Always;
seems only a matter of time.

Forever always waits, for now...

Blue Lotus

Green

Only ever wanted you
happy,
even if I cannot be.
Please forgive
me though,
I can't follow your footsteps
along the merry way.
Told a big fat lie when I said,
I'm not the jealous kind.

Hurts like a bitch
to see you with her;
she seems to wear you better.
Maybe one day,
the bitter part of my sweet heart,
will match the intention
of my honourable spirit.

Can you find her?
Will she fit my glass slipper?
Kiss a million strangers in your quest;
you know you'll never find one that tastes quite like
me...

Let Her Be

Let her
be everything
I could not;
wild,
kinky,
but without
a voice
that can be heard
above yours.

Silly boy!
Blocking me
is not an option,
on the device
that calls
your mind.

EYE SPY...

I saw a picture of you today; for a moment, it took my breath. Then I noticed that you really aren't as handsome as my mind would have me remember. You still have those eyes, the ones that make everyone feel sorry for you. Then I looked at her, and knew it was she who would soon suffocate, and that my sympathy lies, with her.

Sound of Silence

How can you
be bothered
starting over,
telling her
all you told me
as if I was the
first and last
to know?

I guess
human nature
is all about ego;
we never tire
of fresh ears,
hearing our own
voice.

I forgive you for not saying goodbye.
There's far more hope in leaving less sorrow.

Worthy

For you
she pulled
stars
from the sky.

You never
even noticed
the scars
of her endeavor.

Boys don't cry, I heard him say.
Don't listen, I told him.
A real man sheds tears;
it's the only way a woman knows if he is ever worthy,
of hers.

Lucky Stars

Thank heavens
you had the sense
to leave,
before I relinquished
my entire universe,
for an uninhabitable
planet.

*Give me your presence,
not just your word.
I only believe you,
when you lie to my face.*

Mercury

Now,
how do I trust
that any man
with a silver tongue
isn't packing
mercury
in his fangs?

I hate that though barely a man,
you've made me despise them
with such passion, degradation is now
my power.

So Be It

So,
now you take
all of my
broken pieces,
and put yourself
together,
with someone else.

If only we had concluded sooner;
dominant women are not your type.

A Little Less Conversation

I befuddle and confuse
with my dry sense of humour
and sarcastic wit.
To be honest,
I'm not sure
what part of me you ever thought
you liked?
I guess with my mouth busy
and legs open,
I seemed far less complicated.

Disclosed my mind,
unfastened my heart,
let you inside my body.
No, we can't be friends...

Wind Blown

Leave it
to the
Proustian
fragrant
breeze.

Nicotine infused
pages,
vodka kissed
lips,
naïve drugstore
cologne.

Emotional
recall;
scent from the past,
blowing you
back to me.

Box You In

As is the way
these days,
I need to put
you
in a box.

Sociopath,
covert narcissist,
borderline psycho,
toxic egomaniac...

I'm just trying
to figure out
which size I require,
to fit you all in.

Oh,
the lies we make sweet,
to justify the wrong love...

The Dance

Cha-cha
alongside the sun,
never letting on,
you tango
by the moon.

Bodies tangled in mortal sin;
absolved by sacrosanct unification.

Selfless (Look at Me)

Doe eyes,
poised lips,
open just slightly
to suggestion.
Angled from above,
hints of promise
in cleaves of curvature.
Filtered to deconstruct;
unwanted realities,
blurring lines
of imperfection.
Darling,
you're not
fooling anyone;
except yourself.

*Draping melancholy in satin,
smooths her furrows.*

Undisclosed

I never
knew you;
select pieces
you chose
to disclose.

You never
knew me;
willingly
I uncovered
my soul.

*Weaver of intricate lies;
sown with such precision,
no one dares question
your mastery.*

Naked

You stood
naked,
fully-clothed;
exposing
vulnerability
in truth.
I'd never seen
anybody
so beautiful.

I still feel your prints in the dust of our felony.

You Wear It Well

No one guesses
the children
you allowed,
make you small.

The man's
weak spine
you manipulate.

The betrayal
played out.
The neglect
you indulge
by running away.

Karma visits
in those who saw
your broken heart;
only to take.

You wear
it well,
with a dignified
lack of disgrace.

Forever

A fresh daisy
never outlasts
the essence
of a seasoned
wildflower.

*It could only be forever in hidden places,
where loves remains unspoken.*

Case Closed

Revolving doors
offer no closure;
draughts
still tease your back,
hinting
alternative suggestions.

*Just remember,
I'll never allow you the privilege of knowing me again.*

EUPHORIA

The Mad Race

Dated café,
hygiene
questionable.
Appalling service,
I require none.

Vantage point
the highlight.
No one finds me,
cares how much
I order
to justify my seat.

I watch
them scurry;
appointments,
meetings,
schedules.
Wrestling children;
cranky.
Tottering on heels,
far from sexy.

I'm torn,
grateful
not to be required
anywhere
in time.
Sorrowful,
I suspect I'll soon
join their mad race
of validation.

Part of me
longs
to be important.
The better part,
much prefers
to be left
alone.

Bali Awakening

Alley after alley of market stalls,
each offering the same humidity infused garments —
price depending on stupidity and/or compassion.
Please Mrs, this is very rare!
You are my good luck sale for the day!

Spiritual devotion at every turn,
a work ethic to shame us.
Still, I wonder, will they know back home
my Gucci is actually Cucci?
Fifty thousand rupiah is my final offer. *Deal!*

Rats scurry under the counters of food stalls.
I recoil from the offerings on mobile trolleys
wondering if these rodents
are actually the wares on sale?
I watch men fishing in the tranquil stagnation —
my spoilt belly is far too delicate,
my lips too precious, to taste that water.
Don't want to ruin a good time!

Children run bare-footed,
darting between the chaos of city roads,
tap, tapping on car windows —
Quickly lock my door!
Pimped out by their parents for a rupiah or two
these kids are the true entrepreneurs,
not the wealthy westerners in chauffeur driven cars,
concerned for their own unrestrained safety.

The beautician tells tales of no Medicare;
her sick, lost babies.
Chicken is gourmet for her children.
She applies my inferior but cheap eyelashes
as I consider my children's disdain if chicken *is* for dinner.
My eyes sting with tears (or possibly glue).
Can I paint your nails too?
There is only rice this week...

My lashes fall off, one by one.
I hope they are eating chicken.

I return to tourism temple, paradise of westerners.
Vulgar, over-indulged, but always open for a massage or twenty.
The people's smiles seem genuine;
a business tactic, my son reminds me.
Still, happiness is the order of the day amongst the locals,
and I choose to believe.
I'll swallow my Prozac as I sip my cocktail —
depression, it seems,
is a first world problem after all.

Best Laid Plans

She's planning
her journey
on the back
of convention.

Little regard
for those
who came before;
she'll find her way.

Should our paths converge again,
Darling I need you to know,
I no longer see yours,
paved in rose gold.

Wisdom

Come,
sit with me
in the shade
so you don't see,
how much
wiser
I should be.

With age comes only the wisdom that entirely nothing,
is known.

If the Hat Fits

If all the hats fit,
which will I wear
today?
A beanie,
should you choose
to freeze me out?
A sunhat,
in case you burn
with desire?
A helmet;
I may need to dodge
your poison blows.
A tiara,
those rare days
I'm your beguiling
princess.

I'm so damn thankful;
I love hats...

Anarchy

Hold that thought,
lest it scatter
in disarray.
Discombobulating,
short-wiring,
spreading warmth,
popping loudly.

Scramble to regather,
rearrange
to specification.
Always one
insistent on manipulation,
rejoicing in conniption;
anarchy of personality.

*She bears an abstract mind framed by lips
that outline a definitive masterpiece.*

Euphoria

Happy Pill

Why is it not
remotely amusing,
aesthetically pleasing,
more palatable?

Smiley-stamped,
purple polka-dotted,
fairy-floss flavoured;
giggling on the way down...

Indigestible,
gagging reflexes,
sticking in my throat.
The hair of a stranger;
promising grin.
I believe, I must swallow.

Missing in Rhyme

Some days
I pretend
I don't miss you;
distraction
is key.

You'll come back;
you always do...
in those spaces
between seconds,
I'm still busy,
loving you.

*You loved me,
I loved you more.*

*Impossible you said,
but I knew then...*

*And in all since left,
I was right.*

Hummingbird Heartbeat

Persistently
attracted,
nectar
so sweet.

Fluttering
infinity,
long distance
feat.

Skips
for you only;
hummingbird
heartbeat.

We can still be found;
filaments of us,
immortally bound.

Unwritten

Without
your breath
I remain
unwritten.
Typically
your nature
to siphon
as you resuscitate;
disappearing
without sound,
only to leave
words
ringing in my ears.

*I close my eyes now
to see you...*

Moments

There
will be
no goodbye,
there really
was no hello;
just some
moments
in between,
that felt like
forever.

I asked twice for your name
so you'd never guess that I already knew,
I'd never forget it...

Blue Lotus

Back to Myself

Can't feel
you
anymore;
in the new music
I know you'd
despise,
or in the folly
that I'm reading.

Yet,
a smile creeps
around corners
dancing
to the beat,
and I know with certainty
ours will never be;
unwritten.

*My eyes only see you
before final closure,
and after first opening.*

Euphoria

Freed

Don't care
where you are,
what you're doing,
who you're with.

Perplexing;
it tastes metallic.
Like I chewed
through bars,
and found freedom.

*Sometimes,
the lines
become
blurred,
between
pleasure
and pain.*

Belly Laugh

You said,
things always
have a funny way
of working out.

I'll bide my time
waiting for this
heartache to turn
into a belly laugh.

Every day breaking my own heart;
blaming you...

Exorcism

Your spirit rises;
particles and mist,
dissipating
without rolling
down my face.
Relieved of you;
first time ever.

Maybe this is it?
The time you fly away,
and I no longer strain to clutch
at even one feather.

Chakra Chant

Lend to me your chakras,
I intend to unblock every one :

Your crown to acknowledge perfect beauty,
exactly as my eyes do witness.
Your brow the immensity of your intuitive power,
embracing the gift of wondrous imagination.
Your throat unclench as your emotions express,
strangled by years of constriction.
Your siamese-heart unravel, reveal self-love, compassion;
magnetic, to rejoin my own.
Your solar plexus unknot; self-worth and destiny as clear
as it is, to the waiting universe.
Your sacral acceptance of ultimate pleasure and desire,
within divine union of our flesh.
Your root to ground you solidly, as together,
we thrive in survival.

Lie still whilst I open you, one by one.
No need for swinging pendulums or healing hands;
only my energy, my breath, my tongue.

Phoenix

Dispel
our memory,
relegate it
to the ashes
of ancient
mythology.

Rise;
build myself
a new empire
founded on
purity
of truth.

Honour
thyself;
nobility
is in my own
actuality.

*She could equally allow adversity to tarnish her brilliance,
or highlight her unmarred tenacity...*

Adam's Apple

Constricted,
imposed by limitation.
Tentatively inhaling
each small victory,
without obstruction.

Lungs expanding on
e-x-h-a-l-a-t-i-o-n.
Adam's rib
audibly cracking.
Python unravelling;
relishing every bite
of his sweet apple.

*I promise not to step on your toes,
so long as I lead.*

Wasting Time

I've been spending
so much time
measuring
the circumference
of my upper arms
and thighs,
I failed to notice
the way
my new curves
accentuate the size
of my heart.

*Once she reigned in her beauty,
there was no letting go...*

Struggle

The beauty
of transformation
is never truly
appreciated,
without first recognising
the struggle.

*To smell the roses,
one must have first
bled the thorns.*

Unrequited

Pour another glass,
I see euphoria
at the bottom of this bottle.
If not this one,
perhaps jubilation,
comes in red?

Sobriety nothing but
scratchy thorns
to my decaying petals,
fingernails on the blackboard
of my erased spirit.

Sylvia clangs cymbals
in my psyche,
reverberating her mantra:
You've only so long to live,
without a soul to cling to.

Let me go out as all great poets;
grievously short of coronation,
drunk, in unrequited love.
Way before my time.

Between Extremes

My ideal
is tepid,
somewhere
between
the extremes.

Askew
in fruition;
my entire
being
balancing,
on the subtlety
of change.

*Just existing;
somewhere in the void
between not happy or sad...*

One of a Kind

There's no defining
what sets her apart;
her face
symmetrical
as her body lithe,
her heart as wide
as her mind.

*I kept trying to see you beautiful,
but it was only ever a reflection of myself.*

Bare

Strip her bare,
dare to steal her dignity.
Watch how she basks
in vulnerability,
flourishes in defiance
of naked adversity.

Stretch marks are the tattoos our children bestow upon us as an eternal reminder that our hearts have permanently expanded, and our love is forever...

Being

I've not
evolved,
merely
reverted;
into
who I always
was,
before
conditioned
just
to be.

I'm sorry I'm no longer she;
that girl,
content to just be...

Indian Giver

Shun me;
ashamed, agitated,
red-faced.
Disrespect my talent,
feign support
when your guilty conscience
tugs at your
irrepressible ego.

Indian giver,
exponential taker.
I will see you,
nonplussed,
on the other side
of my success.

And so, now I shall remove you
from the words that were never good enough,
and settle for the mediocrity of my success.

Weird

Show me
your weird...

Your
one-of-a-kind
electric rainbow
tutu.

I'm
not interested
in that ripped
denim mask

everyone else
is wearing...

You've become boring, predictable.
Strange...
I thought you were different.

Becoming

Becoming;
middle-aged
woman.

Resenting
every rule
held true,
reconsidering
every thought
owned,
questioning
every belief
entrenched.

Not only
swaying
on edge,
throwing
herself
over.

Undone

In the beginning
she had much to say,
and as sacred,
she kept her
words.

As every other
faltered promise,
they abandon,
letting her go,
undone.

To write is to expose yourself;
a flasher baring your most private parts
to a shocked audience...

Entangled

Even
with weeds
entangled,
she yields
flowers
of undeniable
beauty.

*Learning the art
of unconditionally
embracing
herself...*

Can't Keep a Good Woman Down

You can't
burst my bubble...

I blew it
from lips of steel,
with whimsy,
soap and super-glue.

It's bound
to me by carefully
mastered strings,
of ascending power.

*When you stopped kissing me,
I wonder if again you hoped,
you would take my breath?*

Loving You
(For Kate)

Shame
we move on,
before we let go.

Needing
instant validation,
from yet another.

Scared to learn –
far more to discover,
in love alone.

*Not until the fifth decade,
she breathed herself.
She's spent;
days only exhaling,
to resuscitate everyone else.*

Eden

Her heart beats
in time
with swaying daisies
and hopeful dandelions,
to the melody
of sugar magnolia.
She entertains no weeds,
in her symphony of Eden.

*Caring less for that ho-hum tune,
she rocked her own crazy beat.*

Triumph

Refusing to tip-toe
with trepidation,
embracing imperfection;
dipped and bent.
Scattering tainted velvet
petals into the stratosphere;
showering all,
in her triumphant dance
of victory.

Mystery scent;
leaving only
traces of herself
behind.

Aromatic air
of alluring
wonderment.

Humility

Never lose
your humility.
You're merely
a shiny speck
in the
universal sphere.

Evolution
back into dust,
cares little
for the spotlight
in which
you choose to fall.

*She never commands the spotlight;
it appears uncontrived,
as a mere shadow of her inherent life-force.*

Lotus

She
valiantly
arises
from murk,
astonishingly
cleansed
in purity
of light.

Mystical
goddess,
lunar
deity,
celestial
reverence,
of the
sun.

Each day she emerges;
bathed on moonbeams,
resplendent in light of the sun.

Biographical Note

Leanne Neill is a company director, mother of three, and a self-professed 'composer of words.' She has over twenty years of experience in public libraries and local government. In 2016, she started her poetry and art inspired Facebook page : LUST for WORDS, and has since been published in many ezines and pages including *Spillwords*, *Bymepoetry*, including their WOMb anthology, *The Scarlet Leaf Review*, *Blue Nib*, *Raven Cage*, *Husk Magazine*, and US anthology, *Dandelion in a Vase of Roses*. Her first collection, *Fine Lines and Unpolished Pieces of Me* was published by TAT Publishing in 2017. She lives in Melbourne, Australia.

Find her at :

Facebook.com/LUST-for-WORDS
Instagram : lust_for_words_by_leanne_neill
Twitter : Leanne Neill@LeanneNeill2

- *Blue Lotus* -

www.ingramcontent.com/pod-product-compliance
Lightning Source LLC
Chambersburg PA
CBHW041041110526
R18275900001B/R182759PG44587CBX00001B/1